This is a drama about a man and a bowl of soup.
A drama that is set to music is an opera, so this is…

A Soup Opera

(Please sing this book with passion)

Gmi
What seems to be the prob-lem here?

Waiter:

G7 C
I can't eat the soup!

Man:

Gmi D7/A
What did you say?

Waiter:

G7 C
I can't eat the soup!

Man:

Story and lyrics by Jim Gill
Illustrations by David Moose

Music composed by Steve Rashid and Jim Gill
Orchestration and arrangements by James Falzone

"A Soup Opera," Jim Gill's sing-along opera,
premiered on November 6, 2005 with the
Rockford Symphony Orchestra in Rockford, Illinois.
Steve Larsen was the Music Director and Conductor.

CREDITS FOR CD RECORDING:
Producer: Steve Rashid
Digitally recorded, mixed and mastered at
Woodside Avenue Music Productions, Inc. in Evanston, IL.

MUSICIANS:
Violins: Katherine Hughes, Inger Carle, Carol Kalvonjian
Trumpet: Art Davis
Clarinet: Paul Mertens
Keyboards and Programming: Steve Rashid

VOICES:
Narration by Jim Gill
And (in order of appearance):
Kenneth Donovan, Bradford Newquist,
Angela Stramaglia, Tim Bradley,
James Hamilton, Toni DiDonato.

For information regarding Jim's music and
books for children, contact:
Jim Gill Inc.
PO Box 2263
Oak Park IL 60303-2263
or www.jimgill.com

Library of Congress Control Number: 2008902331
ISBN 978-0-9815721-0-9

Book design by Petertil Design Partners.

Printed and bound in the United States of America.
First edition, 2009; Second edition, 2012

A man walked into one of the finest restaurants in the city and was seated at the very best table.

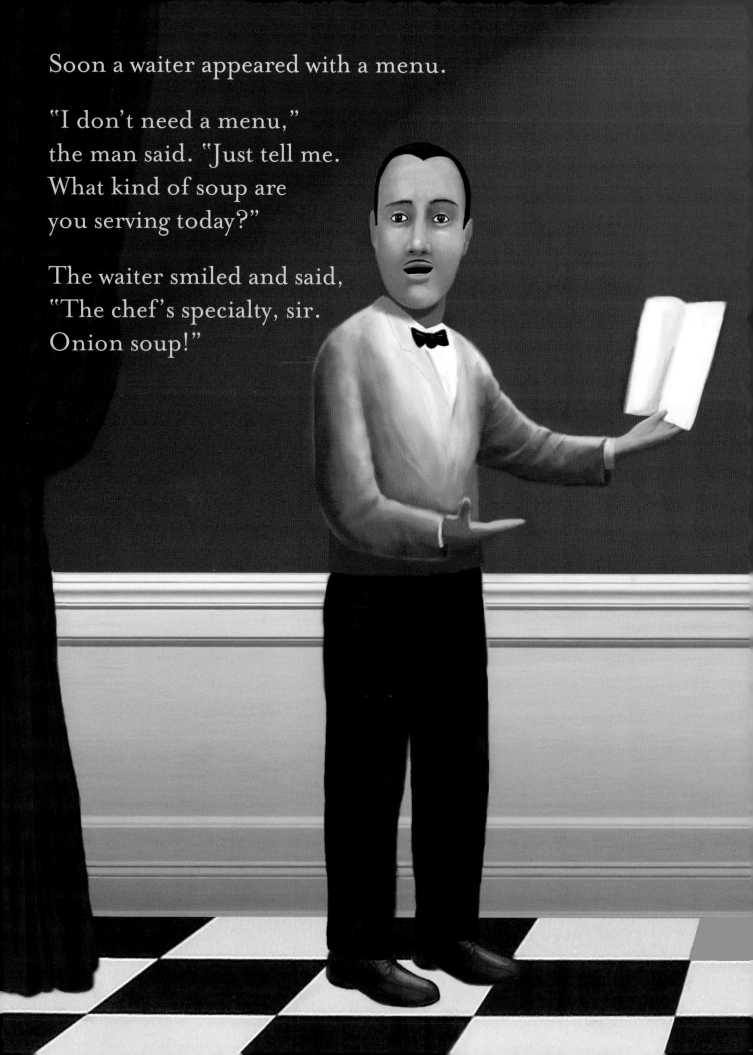

Soon a waiter appeared with a menu.

"I don't need a menu,"
the man said. "Just tell me.
What kind of soup are
you serving today?"

The waiter smiled and said,
"The chef's specialty, sir.
Onion soup!"

"Onion soup sounds delicious,"
said the man.
"I'll take a bowl."

The waiter promptly
returned with a big bowl
of the onion soup.

He set the bowl down
in front of the man.

He turned,
began to walk away,
but was stopped.

"Excuse me," said the man.

The waiter lifted his arms and sang:

What seems to be the problem here?

The man replied: I can't eat the soup!

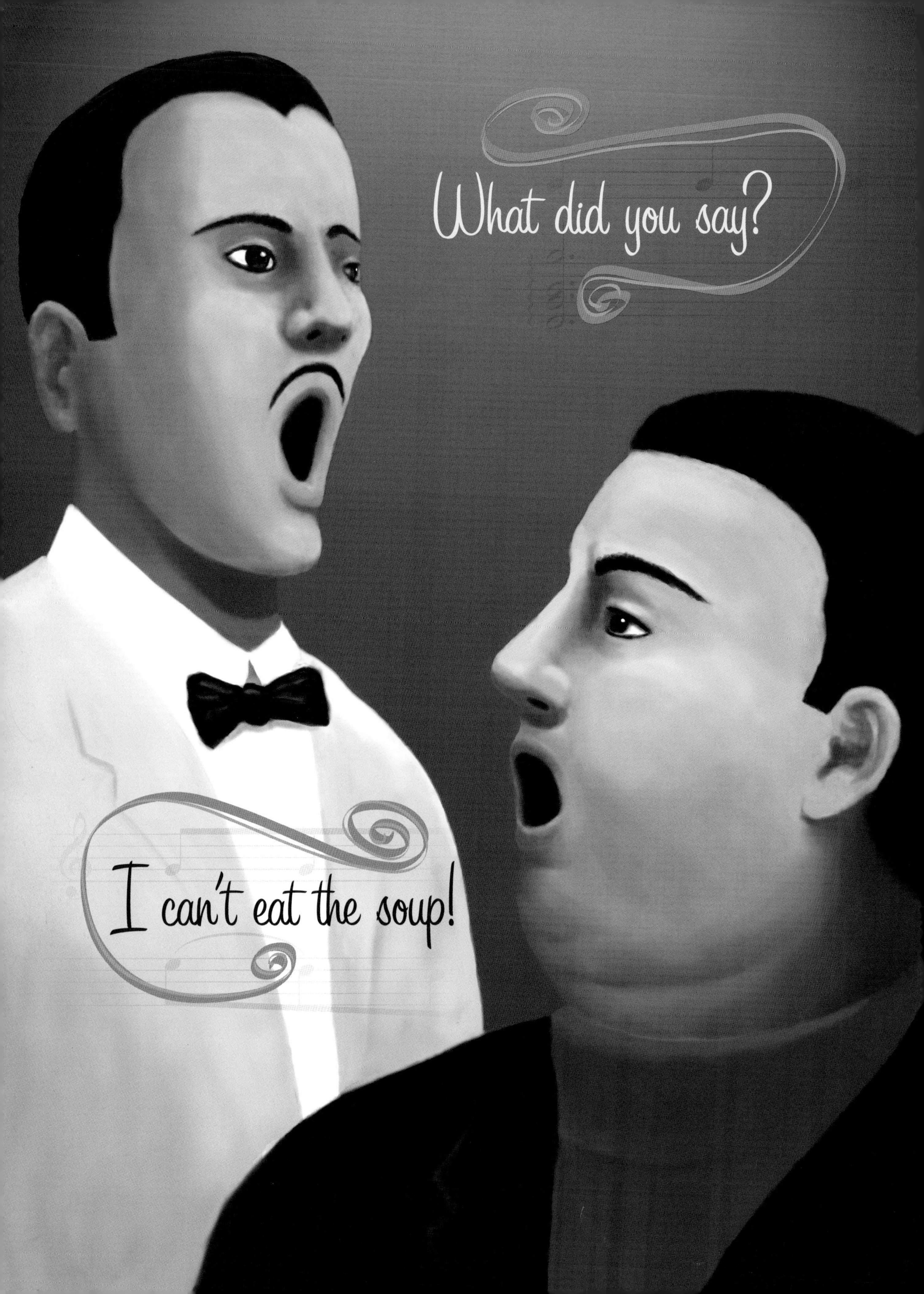
What did you say?
I can't eat the soup!

The waiter scratched his head, thought for a moment
and said, "I'll have to get the chef!"

I can't eat the soup!

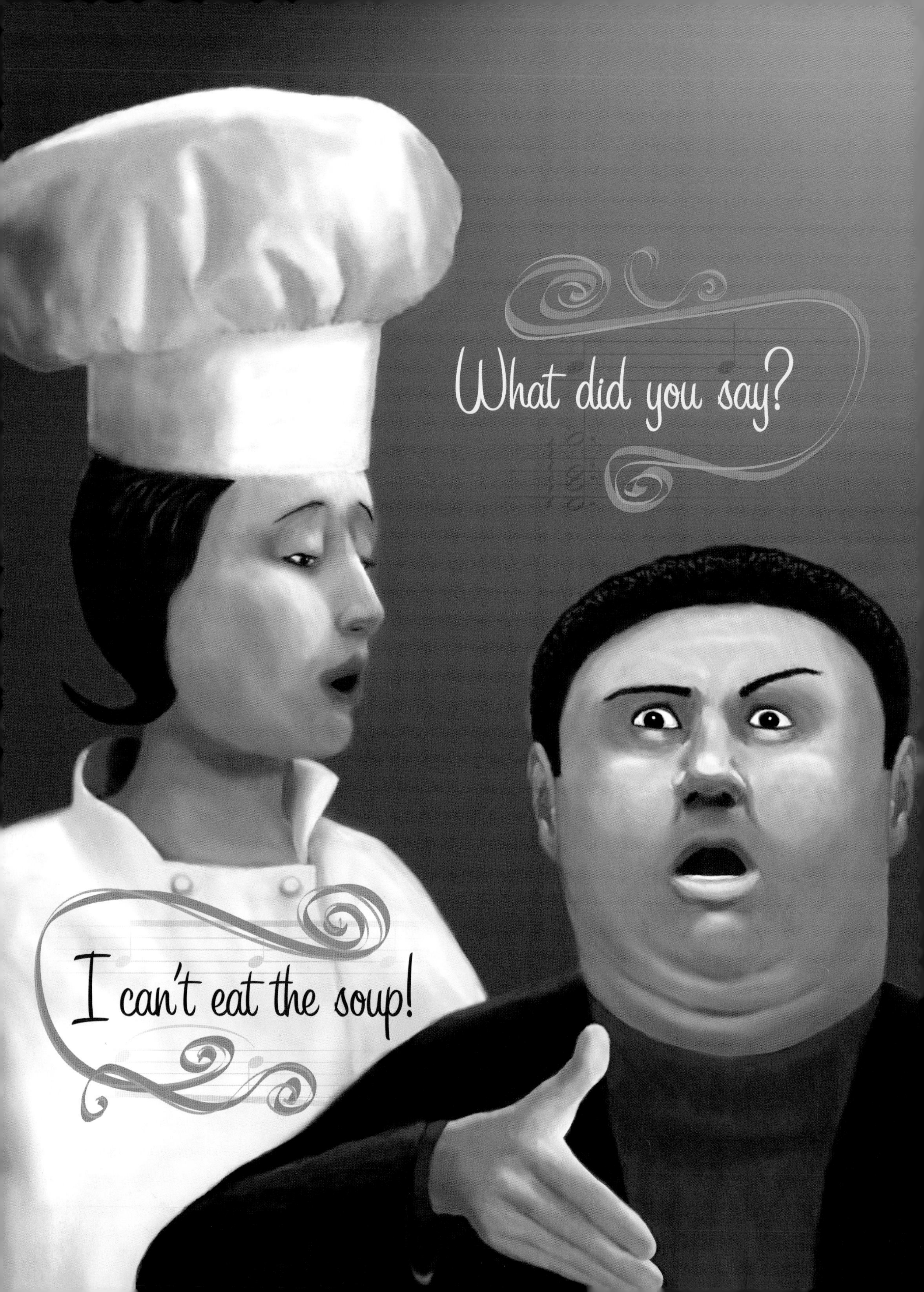
What did you say?
I can't eat the soup!

The chef slapped the ladle in her palm, thought for a moment and said, "I'll have to get a policeman!"

A policeman strolled in wearing a big badge. He sang:

What seems to be the problem here?

I can't eat the soup!

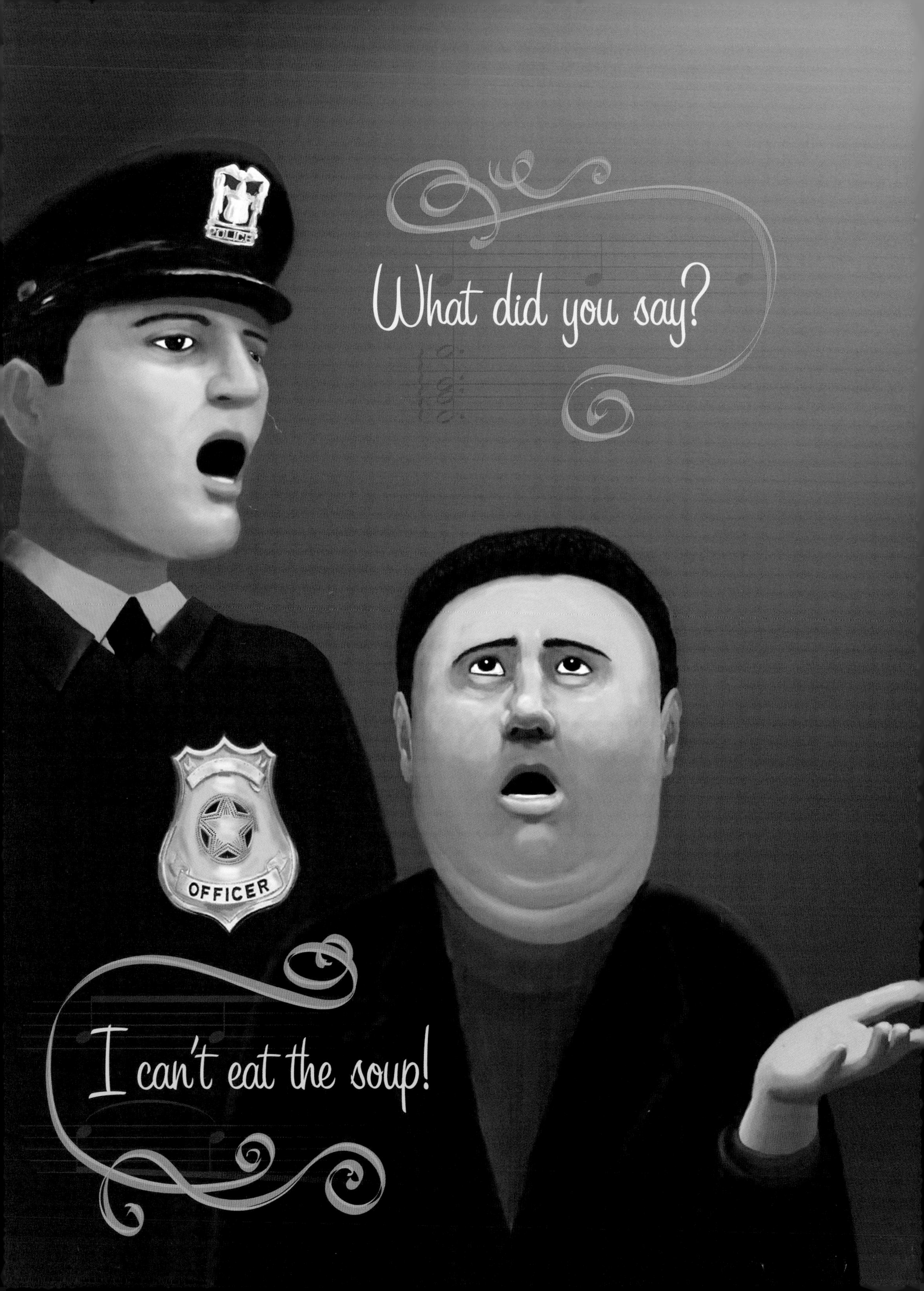
POLICE
What did you say?
OFFICER
I can't eat the soup!

The policeman stroked his chin, thought for a moment and said, "I'll have to get the mayor!"

The mayor stomped in and waved his big pen in the air as he sang:

What seems to be the problem here?

I can't eat the soup!

What did you say?

I can't eat the soup!

The mayor thought for a moment,
pointed a finger in the air and said,
"I'll have to get the President!"

And then the President of the United States walked into the restaurant.

I can't eat the soup!

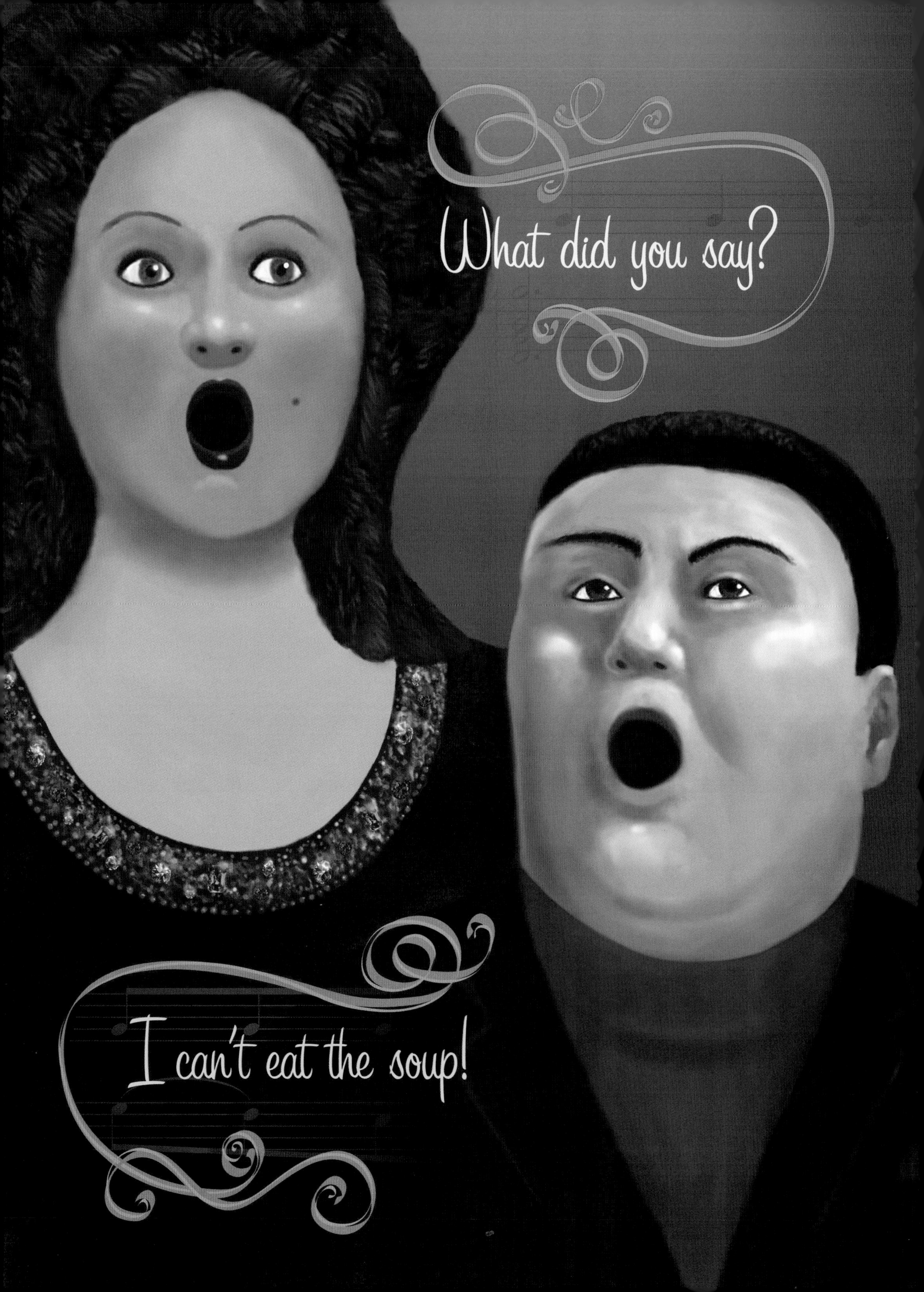
What did you say?
I can't eat the soup!

The President stopped singing and simply asked,
"Why can't you eat the soup, sir?"

Because I have no spoon!